**EDITORIAL TEAM
KIDS MINISTRY PUBLISHING**

**Chuck Peters**
*Director, Kids Ministry*

**Jeremy Carroll**
*Publishing Manager,
VBS and Kids Discipleship*

**Rhonda VanCleave**
*Publishing Team Leader*

**Scott Wiley**
*Writer; Works with preschoolers
in Hermitage, TN*

**Sara Lansford**
*Content Editor*

**Klista Storts**
*Production Editor*

**Gordon Brown**
*Graphic Designer*

Send questions or comments to:
VBS Publishing Team
rhonda.vancleave@li

or by mail to
VBS Publishing Tear
VBS 2023 Babies–2
200 Powell Place, S
Brentwood, TN 37(

or make comments on
www.lifeway.com.

Printed in the United States of America
© 2022 Lifeway Press®

No part of this work may be reproduced or transmitted in any form or by any means, electronic or mechanical, including photocopying and recording, or by any information storage or retrieval system, except as may be expressly permitted in writing by the publisher. Requests for permission should be addressed in writing to:

Kids Ministry Publishing
Lifeway Church Resources
200 Powell Place, Suite 100
Brentwood, TN 37027-7707

ISBN: 9781087772332
Item: 005839247

We believe that the Bible has God for its author; salvation for its end; and truth, without any mixture of error, for its matter; and that all Scripture is totally true and trustworthy. To review Lifeway's doctrinal guideline, please visit www.lifeway.com/doctrinalguideline.

Unless otherwise indicated, all Scripture quotations are taken from the Christian Standard Bible®, Copyright © 2017 by Holman Bible Publishers. Used by permission. Christian Standard Bible® and CSB® are federally registered trademarks of Holman Bible Publishers.

Twists & Turns™ and any other trademarks, service marks, logos, and graphics used herein are the trademarks or registered trademarks or service marks of Lifeway. Other trademarks, service marks, graphics, and logos used in connection with this product may be the trademarks of their respective owners. You are granted no right or license with respect to any of the trademarks or service marks mentioned above or any use of such trademarks or service marks except as specifically stated within this product.

VBS 2023

# TEACHER TIPS

1. Familiarize yourself with the contents of this guide, the *VBS 2023 Babies–2s Leader Pack* (9781087772349), the *VBS 2023 Music for Babies–2s CD* (included in the Leader Pack), and the *VBS 2023 Keepsake Book* (9781087772356).
2. Print the following items to help with planning and preparation: "Planning Chart" (one per teacher), "Child Information Sheet" (one per child), "Parent Update" (one per family), "Hygiene Tips," and "Allergy Alert" (see information below).
3. Prepare all Leader Pack items according to the instructions on each item.
4. Embrace the fact that you are more than a babysitter! The activities in this book are specially designed to help infants through younger 3s learn about God. Choose a few activities to do each day. Don't feel like you need to prepare twenty activities a day to fill the time. Simply choose a few and repeat them throughout the day. Put some away for a while and when you get them back out later, they will be new to the children. It's even OK to repeat activities throughout the week—kids LOVE repetition!

## SAMPLE DAILY SCHEDULE*

- Activities — 80 minutes
- Recreation — 20 minutes
- Snack — 20 minutes
- Rest Time — 30 minutes
- Repeated Activities and Departure — 30 minutes

*For young babies, the daily schedule is determined by the needs of each baby. Feeding, diapering, and meeting basic needs are the top priorities.

## AUDIO RESOURCES

You can find audio resources on the *VBS 2023 Music for Babies–2s CD* in the leader pack or purchase them for download at www.lifeway.com.

## PRINTABLE RESOURCES

These printable teacher helps can be downloaded in the Helps section at https://vbs.lifeway.com/ by clicking on the resources tab.

- Planning Chart
- Child Information Sheet
- Parent Update
- Hygiene Tips
- Allergy Alert
- Hygiene Poster—Changing Diapers
- Cleaning Poster
- Hygiene Poster—Washing Hands
- Sharing God's Plan with Parents

VBS 2023

# SAFETY AND SECURITY TIPS

- ❏ Familiarize yourself with your church's policies and observe all safety and security procedures.

- ❏ Conduct background screenings and check references of every volunteer prior to participating in VBS. (Screening procedures for teachers in kids ministry may be found at www.lifeway.com/backgroundchecks.)

- ❏ Maintain appropriate leader/child ratios (1 leader for every 3 children, with a maximum enrollment of 12, including leaders). Ensure at least 2 leaders are with children at all times.

- ❏ Remove all potential safety and choking hazards from the room. Watch for sharp edges, protruding bolts, and loose items small enough to fit through a paper towel tube (anything that fits is a choking hazard). Cover outlets with safety plugs. Install safety latches on cabinets. Place all cords (including electrical cords and blinds) out of reach. Sit on the floor to get a child's-eye view of the room.

- ❏ Display the "Allergy Alert" outside the room for parents. Each day, list everything kids will touch, smell, or taste.

- ❏ Follow your church's sign-in procedures as parents drop off their children. Obtain a completed "Child Information Sheet" and an emergency number from parents. Pass along any special/allergy information to other leaders.

- ❏ Greet and receive children at the door. For smoother transitions and the security of children already in the room, allow only leaders and children to enter the room.

- ❏ When provided by parents in the child's diaper bag, use only those foods, diapers, wipes, and other supplies.

- ❏ Do not leave a baby unattended on a changing table or in a crib with the rails down.

- ❏ Place babies on their backs to sleep unless directed otherwise by a parent.

- ❏ Assign one leader to every two or three children if the group must leave the room. Insist that children hold the leaders' hands when traveling to a new location. Keep an accurate daily attendance list with you as you travel to make sure everyone is accounted for at all times.

VBS 2023

# HYGIENE AND SNACK TIPS

- ❏ Review guidelines for changing diapers, washing hands, cleaning, and disinfecting on "Hygiene Tips."

- ❏ Post the "Hygiene Poster—Changing Diapers" above changing tables for easy reference by teachers.

- ❏ Post the recipe for disinfecting solution above the sink: 4 cups water + 1 tablespoon chlorine bleach.

- ❏ Prepare fresh disinfecting solution each day. Pour it into a spray bottle (clearly labeled) for easy cleaning of toys and cribs. Keep out of reach of children. Display the "Cleaning Poster" for easy reference by teachers.

- ❏ Clean toys after each use. Every time a child touches or mouths a toy, remove it from the play area until it is cleaned. Wash toys in a dishpan of warm, soapy water; spray them with the disinfecting solution; and rinse them in clear water. Allow toys to air-dry.

- ❏ Wash hands vigorously for at least 20 seconds before feeding a child, before and after treating a cut, after assisting a child with toileting, and after wiping a child's nose or mouth (or your own).

- ❏ Post the "Washing Hands Poster" near the sink as a reminder for teachers.

- ❏ Clean cribs before and after the first session and after each subsequent session. Wipe crib rails, sides, and mattresses with warm, soapy water and spray with disinfecting solution. When dry, put clean sheets on the mattresses.

- ❏ Use caution when allowing children to taste foods approved by (but not provided by) their parents. The following foods should be avoided as choking hazards or potential allergens:
  - Apples (unless peeled and cut into wafer-thin slices)
  - Grapes (can block a child's upper airway when served whole)
  - Hard candy and "gummy" candy
  - Hot dogs
  - Marshmallows
  - Nuts (a common allergen)
  - Oranges (seeds and pulp can present choking hazards)
  - Peanut butter (a common allergen)
  - Popcorn
  - Pretzels
  - Raisins
  - Sunflower and watermelon seeds

## OVERVIEW OF BIBLE STORIES

**Bible Verse:** God loves us. *Psalm 107:1 (paraphrase)*

| DAY 1 | DAY 2 | DAY 3 | DAY 4 | DAY 5 |
|---|---|---|---|---|
| **Bible Story** | **Bible Story** | **Bible Story** | **Bible Story** | **Bible Story** |
| God Made a Beautiful World | God Made Families | God Cared for Noah | Mary and Joseph Heard Good News | Jesus Was Born |
| *Genesis 1:1-31* | *Genesis 2:7-8;16-24; 3:15,20; 4:1-2* | *Genesis 6:9-10; 6:14-22; 7:1,13-19; 8:1-3,13-20* | *Matthew 1:18-24; Luke 1:26-56* | *Luke 2:1-20* |
| **Today's Point** | **Today's Point:** | **Today's Point:** | **Today's Point:** | **Today's Point:** |
| God made everything. | God planned for my family. | God cares for me. | God had a plan for Jesus. | God loves me and sent Jesus. |

### CHRIST CONNECTION

The Bible tells us what is true about God and how we can know more about Jesus.

### LEVEL OF BIBLICAL LEARNING: GOD

God loves people.

*The Levels of Biblical Learning is a tool that reflects levels of understanding at each age that follow how God designed children to learn. For more information visit www.lifeway.com/lobl.*

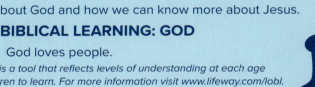

## BIBLE CONTENT

## WHAT IS BIBLE STORY PLUS?

**Bible Story Plus** is a short "group time" type experience for older 2s and younger 3s. It may not occur as a scheduled activity time each day. Instead, it may happen more naturally as you sit on the floor and several children join you of their own accord. This may mean you do Bible Story Plus more than once during the day.

Keep in mind the attention span of the preschoolers in your room and keep group activities short and active. Encourage everyone to join you in the activity, but understand that some children may be ready to move on more quickly than others. It is OK for a child to move to another activity in the room while you continue Bible Story Plus with other children.

**BIBLE STORY PLUS MAY INCLUDE …**

- Telling the Bible Story
- Singing or Moving to Music
- Playing a Game
- Joining in a group activity with friends

# DAY 1 — GOD MADE A BEAUTIFUL WORLD

**Theme Verse:** God loves us. *Psalm 107:1*

**Today's Point:** God made everything.

## BABIES–YOUNGER 1s

*—Based on Genesis 1:1-31*

- God made the world.
- God made the day and the night.
- God made the land and the oceans.
- God made plants and trees.
- God made the sun, moon, and the stars.
- God made all the fish and birds.
- God made all kinds of animals on the land.
- God made people.
- Everything God made is good.

## OLDER 1s–2s

*—Based on Genesis 1:1-31*

In the beginning, God made the world. He made light for the world. God called the light *day*, and He called the darkness *night*.

God made the dry ground and the oceans. God looked at the things He had made. Everything was good.

God said, "Let the land grow all kinds of plants." God made the plants with seed. God saw that what He had made was good.

God made the bright sun to shine in the daytime. He made the moon for the nighttime. God made all the stars. God made fish and ocean animals. God made all the birds.

God made all kinds of animals to live on the land. God made people. God planned for people to take care of the world He made. God looked at the world. Everything He had made was good.

# BIBLE STORY PLUS

**Supplies:** Bible, "Bible Story Picture 1" (pack item 1), "Sorting Cards" (pack item 10)

- Sit on the floor and sing "Play a Game" (Music and Movement Tab). As you sing, gesture to gather preschoolers to sit with you.
- Lay a few of the cards on the floor, picture side up, while continuing the song.
- Say: "I see a dog. Where is the dog?" Flip that card over when identified. Name another picture, identify it, and flip over the card. Say: "Where is the dog?" Encourage children to remember which card is the dog. Flip the card back to the picture side.
- Say: "God made all these things." Open the Bible and tell the Bible story.
- Show "Bible Story Picture 1" (pack item 1).
  Say: "God made everything. Thank You, God!"
- Sing "Thank You, God" (Music and Movement Tab).

## FEEL TEXTURES

**Supplies:** "Bible Story Picture 1" (pack item 1), shallow boxes or box lids, variety of nonpoisonous nature items (such as sticks, smooth rocks, leaves, feather, sand), hot glue gun, orange, potato, carrot, avocado, textured baby toys, hand wipes, "Allergy Alert" (printable resource, see page 2 for instructions)

- Clean all the nature items (as needed). Use hot glue to attach the sticks, rocks, sand, leaves, and feathers to the insides of the boxes, a couple of items in each box. Wash the surfaces of the fruit and vegetables and place them in other boxes. Post an allergy alert by the door of your classroom, informing parents of the items children will touch.
- Arrange boxes on the floor with the picture and toys. Encourage preschoolers to touch the items in the boxes. Talk about the objects and textures they feel.
- Say: "God made everything. God made the trees. God made the rocks. God made the birds."
- Use a wipe to clean a baby's hands when he finishes touching the items.
- **NOTE:** Put nature items out of reach when you cannot supervise their use.

## SHINE A FLASHLIGHT

**Supplies:** Bible, "Book: *Foods I Eat*" (pack item 9), "Sorting Cards" (pack item 10), small nonbreakable flashlights, other books with pictures of nature items or foods, playmat

- Sit on a playmat and arrange the items near you.
- Turn on a flashlight and slowly move the light around the room. When you catch a child's attention, encourage her to take a flashlight and move the light around the room.
- Shine the light on one of the pictures. Say: "God made the sun."
- Encourage children to shine the flashlights on the pictures and books.
- Open the Bible and shine a light on it.
- Say: "The Bible says God loves us. We learn about God at VBS. God made everything. God made you, _____ (insert child's name). God loves you."

## SORT COLORS

**Supplies:** Bible, "Bible Verse Markers" (pack item 7), "Color Gameboard" (pack item 25), "Sorting Cards" (pack item 10), variety of toys and objects in basic colors that match the gameboard, laundry basket

- Place a copy of the "Bible Verse Marker" (pack item 7) in the Bible at Psalm 107:1.
- Gather large interconnecting blocks, large toy cars, plastic cups and containers, and so forth in the six colors that match "Color Gameboard" (pack item 25). Place all these items in the laundry basket. Set the basket near the gameboard. Lay "Sorting Cards" (pack item 10) beside the gameboard, color side up.
- Invite preschoolers to match the objects or color cards to the matching colors on the gameboard.
- As children play, talk about the colors. Say: "Blue. God made a blue sky. God also made birds that are blue."
- Talk about the Bible story. Help a child open the Bible to the marker. Read the verse: "God loves us." Tell the child that he is learning about God at VBS.

## MAKE A MEADOW

**Supplies:** "Bible Story Picture 1" (pack item 1), green construction paper, flower stickers

- Choose the size of the finished meadow and cut the green paper that size. (It can be a full sheet of construction paper, half sheet, or any other size.)
- Offer a preschooler a piece of green construction paper. Help the child peel a sticker and add to his paper. Encourage the child to add more flowers to the meadow.
- Talk about the Bible story as preschoolers work.
- Show a child "Bible Story Picture 1" (pack item 1). Point out flowers or other things God made.
- Say: "God made everything. We can learn about God."
- **NOTE:** Older twos may enjoy using washable markers to add additional details to their meadows.

✷ **EXTEND:** Lead preschoolers to add flower stickers to page 1 of their Keepsake Books. Point to the words on the page as you read "God made everything."

## SCOOP AND POUR SAND

**Supplies:** Large plastic container with sand, drop cloth, smooth river rocks, scoops, small cups

- Spread drop cloth on the floor. Set the container of sand in the middle of the cloth. Hide rocks in the sand.
- Invite preschoolers to scoop, pour, and explore sand.
- Say: "God made the rocks and the land and the mountains. God made everything."
- Talk about the Bible story as children are interested.
- Say: "Thank You, God, for the world You made."
- Sing "Learn About God" (Music and Movement Tab).

# DAY 2

## GOD MADE FAMILIES

**Theme Verse:** God loves us. *Psalm 107:1*
**Today's Point:** God planned for my family.

### BABIES–YOUNGER 1s

—*Based on Genesis 2:7-8,16-24; 3:15,20; 4:1-2*

- God made the world and all the plants and animals.
- The best thing God made was people.
- God made a man and named him Adam.
- God made a woman to help Adam.
- Adam named the woman Eve.
- Adam and Eve had children, Cain and Abel.
- God planned for families.

### OLDER 1s–2s

—*Based on Genesis 2:7-8,16-24; 3:15,20; 4:1-2*

Trees, grass, flowers, birds, cats, and cows—God made everything. The most wonderful things God made were people. The first person God made was a man. God called the man Adam. He put Adam in a beautiful garden named Eden.

God made animals to put in the garden, but none of the animals were the kind of helper that Adam needed. So God made a woman, and Adam named her Eve.

Adam and Eve had children. They had sons named Cain and Abel. Cain and Abel grew just like all children do. God planned for the first family.

# BIBLE STORY PLUS

**Supplies:** Bible, "Bible Story Picture 2" (pack item 2), "Book: *Foods I Eat*" (pack item 9), O-shaped cereal, "Allergy Alert" (printable resource, see page 2 for instructions)

- Sit on the floor with a small cup of cereal. Eat one or two pieces. As children gather, offer each one a few pieces of cereal.
- Show the picture on the back of the book. Say: "We like to eat cereal. Let's see what other foods are in this book." Read the book and note the different food items.
- Say: "Our families give us food to eat. God planned for your families."
- Open the Bible and tell the Bible story. Show "Bible Story Picture 2" (pack item 2) and name the people depicted.
- Pray: "Thank You, God, for families."

## LOOK AT FACES

**Supplies:** Bible, "Bible Verse Marker" (pack item 7), "It's You! Faces" (pack item 11), nonbreakable mirrors, small purses or reusable lunch bags; EXTEND: "It's You! Frames" (pack item 21)

- Mark Psalm 107:1 with a copy of the "Bible Verse Marker" (pack item 7). Place a mirror and one or more of the "It's You! Faces" (pack item 11) in each bag. Lay remaining faces or mirrors on the floor.
- Guide a baby to reach inside a bag and pull out the mirror. Say: "I see your face in the mirror!"
- Talk about the faces on the cards. Point to an adult and say: "This could be a mommy. God made mommies and daddies. God planned for your family. Thank You, God, for _____ 's family." Insert a child's name in the sentence. Repeat, using every child's name.
- Help a child turn the pages in the Bible. When he finds the marker, say: "The Bible says, 'God loves us.' Thank You, God, for loving us."
- ✳ **EXTEND:** Make copies of the "It's You! Frames" (pack item 21). Cut frames apart and attach photos of children in your group to add to the activity. Also add a picture of the child to page 8 of her Keepsake Book.

## ARRANGE ORANGES

**Supplies:** Plastic basket or bowl, 5 oranges, "Bible Story Picture 2" (pack item 2), "Book: *Foods I Eat*" (pack item 9), stacking cups or bowls, "Allergy Alert" (printable resource, see page 2 for instructions)

- Wash the oranges. Place the oranges in the basket or bowl. Lay "Bible Story Picture 2" (pack item 2) on the floor and set the basket of oranges on top of the picture. Lay the book nearby with the stacking cups.
- Invite a child to take the oranges from the basket and place them back in the basket.
- Say: "God planned for your family. Your family gives you good food to eat. Your family takes care of you."
- When a child picks up the picture, talk about the Bible story. Say: "Thank You, God, for our families."
- Talk more about families as children stack cups or look at the book.

NOTE: Use apples or other fruit as desired in this activity. The food used must be hardy enough to withstand handling by young preschoolers. Be prepared to clean the fruit if babies begin mouthing apples.

## FINGER-PAINT

**Supplies:** "Bible Story Picture 2" (pack item 2), nontoxic finger paint, nontoxic scented extracts, small cups, trays, paper, painting smocks, "Allergy Alert" (printable resource, see page 2 for instructions)

- Mix each color of finger paint with one of the scented extracts in a cup. Help a child put on a painting smock. Add finger paint to one of the trays.
- Invite the child to use her hands to paint on the tray.
- Say: "God made people with eyes and ears and noses."
- Show "Bible Story Picture 2" (pack item 2). Talk about the Bible story and the scents children can smell.
- Say: "God made you. You are growing and learning."
- Press a piece of paper on top of the tray to make a print of the child's design. Lift the paper carefully and let dry.

   ✳ **EXTEND:** Help preschoolers add fingerprints or handprints to page 12 of their Keepsake Books.

## PLAY A GAME

**Supplies:** Bible, "Hands and Feet" (pack item 12), colored paper, scissors, tape

- Make copies of "Hands and Feet" (pack item 12) on colored paper and cut apart. Tape copies of four feet (left, right, left, right) to make a path. Tape copies of a left hand and right hand side by side on the floor. Tape left foot and right foot a few inches apart. Tape a few of the hands to a wall at the child's eye level.
- Invite a child to walk or stand on the feet shapes and place her hands on the hand shapes. For older twos, create more combinations of hands and feet.
- Say: "God made you. You are able to do many things."
- Open the Bible to Genesis 1. Point as you say: "God made Adam and Eve. They had a family. God planned for families. God gave you a family, too."
- Sing "Thank You, God" (Music and Movement Tab).

## GROUP PICTURES

**Supplies:** Bible, "Sorting Cards" (pack item 10), "It's You! Faces" (pack item 11), small plastic baskets or bins

- Mix both sets of cards together. Lay them on the floor with the baskets or bins. Sit with the children as they explore the cards. Talk about what you see on the cards.
- Hold a card and say: "I see a picture of a boy. I'll put the boy in this bin." Drop the card in a bin. Choose another card. "This is a tree. This one goes in another bin." Drop in a different bin. Pick up another card. "This is a woman. I will put this one with the boy. These cards go together."
- Help preschoolers group the cards in the bins, or they may randomly drop in and take out cards from the bins.
- Say: "God loves us and made a beautiful world with land animals and fish and trees and people."
- Open the Bible to Psalm 107:1 and read the verse.

# DAY 3 — GOD CARED FOR NOAH

**Theme Verse:** God loves us. *Psalm 107:1*

**Today's Point:** God cares for me.

## BABIES–YOUNGER 1s

—*Based on Genesis 6:9-10,14-22; 7:1,13-19; 8:1-3,13-20*

- Noah loved God.
- God told Noah to build a big boat called an ark.
- God told Noah to take his family and two of every animal into the ark.
- It rained and rained for forty days.
- Noah, his family, and the animals were safe on the ark.
- It stopped raining and the water dried up.
- God told Noah to come out of the ark with all of the animals.
- Noah thanked God for taking care of him and his family.

## OLDER 1s–2s

—*Based on Genesis 6:9-10,14-22; 7:1,13-19; 8:1-3,13-20*

Noah was a good man who loved God. One day God told Noah to build a big boat called an ark.

God also told Noah to take two of every kind of animal with him into the ark. God said it would rain. Noah, his family, and the animals would be safe in the ark.

Noah worked hard to get the ark ready. God told Noah when to get on the ark. Noah's family and all the animals went into the ark.

It rained and rained for forty days. When the rain stopped, Noah waited for the water to dry up. One day God said, "Come out of the ark. Bring your family and the animals with you." Noah thanked God for taking care of him and his family.

# BIBLE STORY PLUS

**Supplies:** Bible; "Bible Story Picture 3" (pack item 3), "Animal Pairs" (pack item 13)

- Sit on the floor and encourage children to gather with you.
- Ask: "What does a lion sound like? Can you make a lion sound?" Encourage children to roar with you. Name other animals for making sounds (dog, cow, frog, cat, pig).
- Say: "God made all kinds of animals. Listen to this Bible story that has all the different animals God made."
- Open the Bible to Genesis 6 and tell the Bible story.
- Show "Bible Story Picture 3" (pack item 3). Ask: "What happened to the animals on the ark?"
- Say: "God took care of Noah and the animals on the ark. God cares for us. God cares for you."
- Show one of the "Animal Pairs" (pack item 13). Name the animal. Say: "Let's pretend to be hippos walking into the ark." Move like a hippo. Repeat with the giraffe, kangaroo, and camel.
- Say: "I'm glad we can learn about God. The Bible tells about God. Thank You, God, for the Bible."

## HAMMER ON BLOCKS

**Supplies:** "Bible Story Picture 3" (pack item 3), toy plastic hammers, cardboard blocks or shoeboxes, baby hammering toys

- Arrange items on the floor. Gently tap a hammer on one of the blocks.
- Invite a child to use the hammer and the blocks.
- Say: "God told Noah to build a big boat called an ark." Talk about the Bible story.
- When a child picks up the picture, talk about what he sees.
- Say: "God cared for Noah. God cares for you, too. Thank You, God, for loving and helping us."

✱ **EXTEND:** Take photos of the children to add to pages 8–9 of the Keepsake Books.

## PLAY WITH ANIMALS

**Supplies:** Bible, "Bible Verse Marker" (pack item 7), "Animal Pairs" (pack item 13), medium-size box, large plastic animals, tape, scissors

- Cut apart "Animal Pairs" (pack item 13) and tape them to the sides of the box. Set the box on the floor and arrange animals around it. Place a couple of animals inside the box.
- Place a "Bible Verse Marker" (pack item 7) in the Bible at Psalm 107:1. Set the Bible near the box.
- Talk about the animals as a child holds the toy figures.
- Say: "God told Noah to build a big boat called an ark."
- Encourage preschoolers to put the animals in the box and push the box around.
- Talk more about the Bible story. Say: "God cared for Noah and the animals on the ark. God cares for you, too. We can learn about God."
- Help a child open the Bible as you say the verse.

DAY 3      BABIES–YOUNGER 1s • BIBLE ACTIVITIES

## SPRAY WATER

**Supplies:** "Bible Story Picture 3" (pack item 3), empty leader pack bag, spray bottles with water, plastic toy boat, plastic dishpan or large bin, towels

- Slide "Bible Story Picture 3" (pack item 3) into the empty leader pack bag to keep it dry. Seal the bag. Spread a towel on the floor. Set the dishpan or bin in the middle of the towel. Place the toy boat in the dishpan. Set the spray bottles nearby but out of reach of preschoolers until they are needed.
- Hand a spray bottle to a child. Show him how to spray water onto the boat or in the dishpan beside the boat.
- As children spray water, talk about the Bible story. Say: "God told Noah to build a big boat called an ark. Noah's family and the animals went inside the ark. The rain came. Rain fell for forty days."
- Show the Bible story picture as you say: "God cared for Noah and the animals on the ark. God cares for you."

**EXTEND:** For older twos, put about 1 inch of water in the dishpan. Encourage the twos to float toy boats or pat the water to make waves.

## BUILD AN ARK

**Supplies:** "Animal Pairs" (pack item 13), "Bible Verse Markers" (pack item 7), large box (will be used again on Day 4), plastic toy hammers and other tools, cardboard blocks, tape, 4 shoeboxes or oatmeal boxes, scissors; EXTEND: Crayons, *VBS 2023 Theme Stickers* (9781087776552)

- Cut apart "Animal Pairs" (pack item 13) and tape one of each pair to a shoebox or oatmeal box so the picture will stand. Tape 2–3 copies of the "Bible Verse Markers" (pack item 7) to sides of the large box.
- Invite a child to explore the materials and play as she chooses. Comment: "We can build an ark. An ark is a large boat. God told Noah to build an ark."
- Preschoolers may want to use the tools on the box. They can stack blocks or pretend to use tools.
- Call attention to the animal pictures. Say: "God told Noah to take animals onto the ark."
- As a child hammers on the box, point to the words of the verse. Say: "These words say, 'God loves us.' At VBS we learn God loves us. God cares for you and me."

✱ **EXTEND:** Add crayons and stickers for children to decorate the box or lay the box on one side so they can go through it.

# DAY 4

# MARY AND JOSEPH HEARD GOOD NEWS

**Theme Verse:** God loves us. *Psalm 107:1*

**Today's Point:** God had a plan for Jesus.

## BABIES—YOUNGER 1s

*—Based on Matthew 1:18-24; Luke 1:26-56*

- God sent an angel to talk to Mary.
- The angel said God chose Mary to have a baby.
- God sent an angel to talk to Joseph in a dream.
- The angel told Joseph about Mary's baby.
- The baby's name would be Jesus.
- The angel said that Jesus would help all people.
- Mary and Joseph did what God told them to do.

## BIBLE STORY FOR 2s

*—Based on Matthew 1:18-24; Luke 1:26-56*

God sent an angel to talk to a young woman named Mary. The angel said, "God has chosen you to be the mother of a special baby boy. His name will be Jesus."

Mary said, "I will do what God wants me to do." The angel left Mary.

Mary was going to marry a man named Joseph. Joseph was a kind man who did things that were right.

One night, while Joseph was sleeping, God sent an angel in a dream. The angel said, "Mary is going to have a baby. The baby is God's Son. You will name Him Jesus. He will help all people."

When Joseph awoke he remembered his dream. Joseph did what God told him to do. Joseph and Mary were married. They waited for the day Jesus would be born.

DAY 4        17        BIBLE STORY

# BIBLE STORY PLUS

**Supplies:** Bible; "Bible Story Picture 4" (pack item 4), "Jesus Cube" (pack item 15), large plastic bowl, *VBS 2023 Music for Babies–2s*

- Sit on the floor. Place the bowl about an arm's length from you. Toss the "Jesus Cube" (pack item 15) into the bowl. Retrieve the cube and toss it again.
- Encourage boys and girls to take turns tossing the cube into the bowl.
- Lead the children to sit with you. Show the picture of Mary and Joseph on the cube. Say: "Mary and Joseph heard something that was surprising."
- Set the cube aside and open the Bible. Tell the Bible story.
- Show "Bible Story Picture 4" (pack item 4).
- Say: "God had a plan. Jesus would be born. Mary and Joseph would take care of Baby Jesus."
- Play "Families Love." Clap as you sing.

## CARE FOR A BABY

**Supplies:** Bible, "Jesus Cube" (pack item 15) plastic baby dolls, small baby blankets, shoeboxes or bins (to be used as doll beds); EXTEND: Nontoxic finger paint, foam paintbrushes, hand wipes

- Prepare the cube and arrange items on the floor.
- Help a child wrap a doll in a blanket. Talk about the Bible story.
- Say: "God told Mary she would have a baby. The baby would be Jesus."
- Talk about ways that parents take care of babies.
- Say: "God had a plan for Jesus. Mary and Joseph took care of Him."
- Look at the pictures on the cube. Find the pictures of Mary and Joseph.
- Help a child turn the Bible pages. Say: "God loves us. We learn about God's love for us in the Bible."

**✳ EXTEND:** Help children make footprints on page 13 of their Keepsake Books. Comment: "You were a baby. Now you are growing bigger."

## LISTEN TO SHAKERS

**Supplies:** "Bible Story Picture 4" (pack item 4), "Twists & Turns Clip Art" (pack item 8), clear plastic drink bottles with lids, glue, tape, rice, jingle bells, small plastic number cubes, aquarium gravel, *VBS 2023 Music for Babies–2s*

- Make shakers by adding the different items to separate plastic bottles. Seal the lids with glue and tape. Make copies of the "Twist & Turns Clip Art" (pack item 8). Tape one strip around each bottle. Set the shakers on the floor around "Bible Story Picture 4" (pack item 4).
- Guide a child to shake one of the bottles. Say: "You can hear the sounds. The cubes rattle inside the bottle."
- Point to the picture. Say: "Mary and Joseph heard good news. God sent an angel to each of them to tell them about His plan. God had a plan for Jesus."
- Sing "Special Jesus" as the children shake the shakers.

DAY 4 · BABIES–YOUNGER 1s · BIBLE ACTIVITIES

## MAKE A STAR PICTURE

**Supplies:** "Jesus Cube" (pack item 15), paper, star stamps, washable ink pads or shallow pans of paint, hand wipes, painting smocks

- Show children how to press stamps into the ink pads or paint and make star shapes on paper.
- Encourage the children to make stars all over their papers.
- Talk about things people do at night (brush teeth, sleep, etc.).
- Say: "One night Joseph was sleeping. An angel talked to him in a dream. Joseph heard that Mary would have Baby Jesus."
- Find the picture of Joseph on the cube. Talk about the other pictures on the cube. Say: "God had a plan for Jesus."
- Clean hands when a child finishes his picture.

**EXTEND:** Take photos of the children as they work. Add the photos to pages 8–9 of the Keepsake Books.

## READ BOOKS AND BIBLES

**Supplies:** Bibles; "Bible Pictures" (pack item 14); "Book: *Foods I Eat*" (pack item 9); large box; quilt or blanket; books about Jesus, babies, or families

- Lay a large box on its side. (Use the "ark" box from Day 3, if available.) Spread a quilt or blanket in the bottom of the box and out onto the floor in front of the opening. Insert each "Bible Picture" (pack item 14) into a Bible. Arrange the Bibles and books in the box or around the opening.
- Encourage children to sit in the box or on the quilt and look at the books.
- Point to pictures and talk about what you see.
- Say: "The Bible tells us about God. We can learn about God at VBS. God sent an angel to tell Mary good news." Talk about the Bible story.
- Find the picture with Mary in one of the Bibles and show the children. Talk about other parts of the Bible story (or preview the Day 5 story) when children find the other Bible pictures.

## LISTEN AND MOVE

**Supplies:** "Bible Story Picture 4" (pack item 4); colorful scarves, napkins, or bandannas; *VBS 2023 Music for Babies–2s*

- Give each child a scarf or bandanna. Show children how to hold the scarf by an edge or corner and wave it in the air.
- Sing "Up and Down" (Music and Movement Tab) and guide children to move the scarves up and down with the song. Some may wave randomly. Others may just stand and hold scarves. Let them participate as they choose.
- Play the "Twists and Turns" theme song. Allow children to move around the room with the music. They can wave the scarves, or you can gather them for later.
- Play other songs for children to move.
- Say: "You can hear the music. Do you know what Mary heard? She heard an angel's voice tell her she would have a baby!" Look at "Bible Story Picture 4" (pack item 4).

**EXTEND:** Take photos of the children with the scarves. Add the photos to pages 8–9 of the Keepsake Books.

# DAY 5 — JESUS WAS BORN

**Theme Verse:** God loves us. *Psalm 107:1*

**Today's Point:** God loves me and sent Jesus.

## BABIES–YOUNGER 1s

*—Based on Luke 2:1-20*

- Joseph and Mary went to Bethlehem.
- Joseph found a place for Mary to rest.
- Soon Baby Jesus was born.
- Mary wrapped the special baby in soft cloths.
- She laid Him in a manger bed.
- Shepherds heard that Baby Jesus was born.
- The shepherds hurried to see Him and thanked God for Jesus.

## OLDER 1s–2s

*—Based on Luke 2:1-20*

Mary, Joseph, and many other people went to Bethlehem. The inn was full. But Joseph found a place where they could rest.

Soon Baby Jesus was born. Mary gently wrapped Him in soft cloths to keep Him warm. She laid Jesus in a manger. A manger was a feeding bin for animals. Mary and Joseph took special care of the tiny Baby Jesus.

Shepherds heard that Baby Jesus was born. They hurried to see Him. They thanked God for the special baby. Mary, Joseph, and the shepherds were happy that Jesus was born.

# BIBLE STORY PLUS

**Supplies:** Bible; "Bible Story Picture 5" (pack item 5)
*VBS 2023 Music for Babies–2s*

- Play "Twists and Turns" theme song. March around the room and encourage children to follow you as you march.
- Sit down when the song ends and gather children around you.
- Say: "We can learn about God at VBS. What a fun time we have had! One thing we can learn is God loves you! And you and you and you!" (Point to the children.)
- Say: "God loves us, and He sent Jesus."
- Open the Bible and tell the Bible story.
- Show "Bible Story Picture 5" (pack item 5). Encourage the children to point to Jesus.
- Sing "Thank You, God" (Music and Movement Tab), substituting *Jesus* for *the sun*.

## EXPLORE A DIAPER BAG

**Supplies:** Bible, "Jesus Cube" (pack item 15), diaper bag, blanket, rattle, other baby toys; EXTEND: Crayons

- Place blanket, rattle, and "Jesus Cube" (pack item 15) inside the diaper bag. Set the Bible on the floor and place the diaper bag next to it. Arrange other toys around the Bible.
- Invite a child to look inside the bag. She may want to pull all the items out of the bag.
- Say: "God sent Jesus. Jesus was a baby." Show the picture on the cube.
- Encourage children to play with the toys or fill the diaper bag with them.
- Open the Bible and say: "God loves us. We can learn that God loves us and cares about us. God loves you!"

✳ **EXTEND:** Mention the children's families. Offer a crayon for a child to draw his family (or make crayon marks) on page 5 of the Keepsake Book.

## ROLL A BALL

**Supplies:** "Bible Pictures" (pack item 14), inflatable ball, clear page protectors, wide clear tape; EXTEND: "Bible Story Pictures" (pack items 1–5) (consider laminating for extra durability)

- Slide each of the "Bible Pictures" (pack item 14) into a page protector. Lay the pictures in a line on the floor. Tape around all four sides of each picture, securing the page protector to the floor. Set the inflated ball nearby.
- When a child shows interest, roll the ball over the pictures. Then roll the ball to the child. Encourage him to roll it over the pictures.
- Continue to play the game as the child chooses.
- Point to the pictures and talk about each one.
- Say: "God loves us and sent Jesus. God loves you, _____." Insert each child's name in the sentence.

**EXTEND:** Tape all the Bible Story Pictures (pack items 1–5) to the floor. Review the Bible stories when a child shows interest in the pictures.

## TALK ABOUT THINGS BABIES NEED

**Supplies:** "Bible Pictures" (pack item 14), "Black and White Designs" (pack item 22), plastic baby dolls, baby blankets, diaper bags, rattles, small empty lotion bottles or powder bottles, other baby toys, white heavyweight paper, large binder rings, hole punch; EXTEND: Toy bottles, other baby care items, "Book: *Foods I Eat*" (pack item 9)

- Make copies of "Black and White Designs" (pack item 22) onto white heavyweight paper. Cut the designs apart, punch a hole in an upper corner, and place several designs on a binder ring to make a baby book. Make several books.
- Place one of the homemade books and a few items in each diaper bag. Lay other books and items on the floor.
- Suggest the children take care of the baby dolls. Talk about the things that babies need.
- Say: "God loves us, and He sent Jesus."
- Show the picture of Baby Jesus. Mention things that Mary probably did to care for Jesus.
- Use the other pictures to talk about other parts of the Bible story.
- Say: "We can learn about God. God loves you."

**EXTEND:** For older twos, add toy bottles and other baby care items. Include "Book: *Foods I Eat*" (pack item 9). Talk about how parents care for babies and preschoolers.

## STACK AND BUILD

**Supplies:** Bible, "Jesus Cube" (pack item 15), "Animal Cube" (pack item 16), "Color Cube" (pack item 17), "Pattern Cube" (pack item 18), cardboard blocks, other appropriate building toys

- Prepare the cubes.
- Lead preschoolers to stack the blocks and cubes.
- Open the Bible and say: "God loves us. Today we can learn that God loves us and sent Jesus."
- Talk about the story of Jesus' birth and challenge a child to find a cube with pictures about this Bible story.

**EXTEND:** Roll the "Color Cube" (pack item 17). Ask preschoolers to find something that color to add to the structure.

## DRESS IN BIBLE TIMES CLOTHES

**Supplies:** "Bible Story Picture 5" (pack item 5), small Bible times clothes or child-size robes

- Talk about the clothing when children show interest.
- Help them put on the robes or other clothing items.
- Say: "You look like Mary. You look like a shepherd."
- Look at "Bible Story Picture 5" (pack item 5) and talk about the Bible story.
- Say: "God loves us, and He sent Jesus. Thank You, God for Jesus!"

**EXTEND:** Take photos of the children in the Bible times clothing. Add the photos to pages 8–9 in the Keepsake Books.

## WHAT ARE THEME ACTIVITIES?

The activities in this section of the book relate to the overall theme and Bible content of VBS. Unlike the previous "Bible activities," theme activities do not necessarily relate to a specific Bible story. But they're not "just for fun." They are still designed to help you teach Bible truths in ways that are meaningful and applicable to young children. Choose 2–3 of these activities to use in addition to the Bible activities each day. You may choose to use different activities each day or repeat activities throughout the week of VBS. It's totally up to you! Each page is labeled across the bottom to help you know which activities are designed for babies–younger 1s and which are for older 1s–2s.

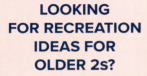

**LOOKING FOR RECREATION IDEAS FOR OLDER 2s?**

Check out the other side of this page!

THIS ICON INDICATES THAT AN ACTIVITY USES THE

**VBS 2023 KEEPSAKE BOOK** (9781087772356). This book makes a great souvenir from the week! Ideas for using the Keepsake Book are available on the inside back cover of this book.

# THEME ACTIVITIES

# RECREATION IDEAS

## Follow a Game Path
**Supplies:** Colorful buckets, pails, and cones
- Arrange the buckets and cones in a line or zigzag path in the play area. Invite preschoolers to walk or move around the buckets and cones. They can weave between them and walk around them as if they were walking on a game path.

## Find the "Checkers"
**Supplies:** Plastic plates or flying discs, plastic bin or dishpan
- Scatter the plates or flying discs around the play area.
- Lead preschoolers to look around the area and gather all the large "checkers" as they find them.
- They can drop the plates/discs into the plastic bin.
- Other preschoolers may enjoy "hiding" the checkers again for friends to gather.

## Move the Parachute
**Supplies:** Play parachute, colorful paper wads (optional)
- Spread the parachute on the play area. Guide preschoolers to sit around the parachute.
- Pick up the parachute by the edges; tell children to pick up the parachute sides, too. Move the parachute up and down together.
- Sing "Up and Down" (Music and Motions Tab) as you move the parachute.
- For older twos, place a couple of paper wads on the parachute and then move it up and down.
- Drop the parachute and gather the paper wads when they fly from the parachute.

## Pretend to be Spinners
**Supplies:** Plastic hoops
- Encourage two preschoolers to hold onto a hoop with you.
- Walk in a circle, around and around, as you hold onto the hoop. (Do not try to walk fast. Allow children to set the pace.)
- For older twos, encourage them to spin around independently. Children may also enjoy exploring other play with the hoops.

## Other Quick Ideas
- Push walking toys or pull wagons along a chalk game path.
- Watch and chase bubbles.
- Toss beanbags into a laundry basket.
- Pretend to be lions, dogs, and other animals.

## DROP GAME CARDS IN A BOX

**Supplies:** "Game Cards Printable" (pack item 19), heavyweight paper, game cards collected from board or card games, empty tissue boxes, colored tape, scissors, playmat, colored contact plastic (optional)

- Make copies of the "Game Cards Printable" (pack item 19) on heavyweight paper and cut the cards apart. Tape around the "mouth" of the tissue boxes. If you choose, cover the tissue boxes with contact plastic. Place the cards and the boxes on the playmat.
- Sit near the boxes. Drop a card into one of the boxes to gain preschoolers' attention.
- Invite preschoolers to drop the cards into the boxes or take them out of the boxes.
- Say: "Families play and have fun together. God gave us families to care for us."

**✻ EXTEND:** Help a preschooler glue a few game cards or paper squares onto pages 14–15 of the Keepsake Book.

## USE A PICTURE SPINNER

**Supplies:** "Sorting Cards" (pack item 10), lazy Susan turntables, tape

- Tape a few of the "Sorting Cards" (pack item 10) on each turntable.
- Place the turntables on the floor.
- Sit with a baby and gently turn a turntable. When the baby pats the turntable, stop and talk about the picture. Say: "This is a dog. God made animals. God made everything."
- Encourage 1-year-olds to turn the turntables themselves.
- Sing "Thank You, God" (Music and Movement Tab) as preschoolers explore the pictures on the turntables.

DAYS 1–5

## CRAWL ON A STICKY GAME PATH

**Supplies:** "Bible Story Pictures 1–5" (pack items 1–5), "Large Gameboards" (pack item 24), tape, clear contact plastic

- Make copies of the "Large Gameboards" (pack item 24) as needed. Tape two of the "Bible Story Pictures" (pack items 1–5) and a few gameboards in a row on the floor to make a "game path." Cut lengths of contact plastic and lay the plastic with the sticky side up over the game path. Tape all the sides of the contact plastic to the floor so the pictures are visible underneath. Make a couple of game paths if space allows.
- Encourage a child to touch the sticky paper.
- Say: "This is sticky. Can you feel it?"
- Invite children to crawl or walk on the sticky game path. Hold the hand of any walking child.
- Call attention to a Bible story picture and say: "We can learn about God at VBS."

## FLIP AND FIND PICTURES

**Supplies:** Bible, "It's You! Faces" (pack item 11), "It's You! Frames" (pack item 21), heavyweight paper, photos of children from class, homemade flipboard (see "Instructions" [pack item 20])

- Take photos of the children in your class. Make copies of the "It's You! Frames" (pack item 21) and add the photos to the frames. Use these photos and the "It's You! Faces" (pack item 11) to put underneath the flaps of your homemade flipboard. Several flipboards may be created.
- Encourage a child to flip up the flap and discover the picture underneath.
- Say: "You can find faces in this game. You found a face that is wearing a hat."
- When a child finds a friend's photo, say: "You found _____ (insert child's name from the photo)! God loves _____ (same child's name)! God loves you, _____ (insert child's name who opened the flap)."
- Open the Bible to the Bible verse. Say: "God loves us. You can learn about God's love at VBS."

**EXTEND:** Duplicate photos of the preschoolers and add to pages 8–9 of the Keepsake Books.

DAYS 1–5

## EXPLORE WATER SENSORY BOTTLES

**Supplies:** Plastic drink bottles, small plastic number cubes, small game pieces, water, light corn syrup, buttons, small loom bands, funnel, glitter (optional), food color (optional), glue, tape

- Make water sensory bottles. Fill some bottles about halfway with corn syrup. Drop in a combination of loom bands, game pieces, and number cubes. Add glitter if you choose. Add water to the bottle, almost filling it; leave some space at the top for movement. Fill other bottles about ¾ with water. Drop in a combination of buttons, game pieces, and number cubes. Add food color to create different colors of water. Seal the lids of all bottles with glue and tape.
- Guide a younger preschooler to hold, roll, shake, or tilt a bottle. Talk about what you see inside the bottles.
- Sing "Learn About God" (Music and Movement Tab).
- Say: "We can learn about God at VBS. God loves and cares for you."

## STACK AND TOSS

**Supplies:** "Jesus Cube" (pack item 15), "Animal Cube" (pack item 16), "Color Cube" (pack item 17), "Pattern Cube" (pack item 18), large sponges, large plastic bin

- Set the cubes and sponges near the bin.
- Invite a child to stack the sponges or the cubes.
- Show children how to toss the cubes or sponges into the bin.
- Point to a picture on the "Animal Cube" (pack item 16). Say: "God made cats. God made animals. God made everything. Thank You, God."

DAYS 1–5

## DECORATE A GAMEBOARD

**Supplies:** "Large Gameboards" (pack item 24), washable paint or washable stamp pads, painting smocks, wipes

- Make copies of the "Large Gameboards" (pack item 24) so each child will have one if he chooses.
- Show a child how to press his fingers in the paint or stamp pad and then onto the gameboard.
- Encourage him to make designs as he chooses with his fingers and the paint or stamp pad.
- Say: "God made you. God made your fingers and your hands. God loves you."
- Sing "God Loves and Cares" (Music & Movement Tab).

**EXTEND:** Help the child make fingerprints on page 12 of his Keepsake Book.

## PLAY IN A TUNNEL

**Supplies:** "Sorting Cards" (pack item 10), large box, masking tape

- Open the top and bottom flaps of the box and lay it on its side. Tape a few of the sorting cards, color side out, inside the box. Use masking tape to create a game path into the box (on both ends of the tunnel).
- Encourage a child to crawl on the game path and into the tunnel.
- Point to the color side of a "Sorting Card" (pack item 10). Say: "Green. God made green grass. God made green frogs. God made everything."

**EXTEND:** Tape a "Bible Story Picture" (pack items 1–5) inside the box for preschoolers to discover. Talk about the Bible story.

**Option:** Instead of a box, use a small table. Drape a tablecloth over two sides of the table, leaving the other two sides open for the tunnel.

DAYS 1–5 • BABIES–YOUNGER 1s • THEME ACTIVITIES

## STACK RINGS

**Supplies:** "Twists & Turns Clip Art" (pack item 8), "Black and White Designs" (pack item 22), paper plates, plastic cups, baby ring toys, tape, scissors

- Cut the middles from paper plates to make rings large enough for rings to fit over a plastic cup. Make copies of the "Twists & Turns Clip Art" (pack item 8). Cut clip art strips and tape around the cups. Set cups on the floor, open side down.
- Cut, fold, and tape the "Black and White Designs" (pack item 22). Set one of the trifold designs on each cup and secure with tape.
- Help a child place a ring over one of the cups. Encourage her to continue to place rings on the cups.
- Say: "You are growing and can do many things. God made you, _____ (insert child's name). God loves you. You can learn about God."
- Sing "Play a Game" (Music and Movement Tab) as the children explore the rings and ring toys.

**EXTEND:** Help children place flower stickers in the Keepsake Books on page 1. Suggest children add flower stickers to the paper plate rings, too.

## TOUCH MOBILES

**Supplies:** "Black and White Designs" (pack item 22) trifolds, chenille stem loops, black and white ribbons, embroidery hoops, yarn, *VBS Music 2023 for Babies–2s*

- Assemble the "Black and White Designs" (pack item 22) trifolds. Make mobiles. Tie a variety of black and white ribbons to an embroidery hoop. Tie a couple of the trifolds to ribbons on each mobile. Hang the mobiles with yarn.
- Hold a child so he can touch the ribbons. Say: "Feel the ribbons. Your hands can touch and feel."
- Lie or sit under a mobile with a child. Look up at the designs. Say: "See the black and white. God made you. God loves you."
- Sing "I Am Safe."

DAYS 1–5

## FIND THE BIBLE

**Supplies:** Bibles, "Bible Verse Markers" (pack item 7), "Color Gameboard" (pack item 25), small blanket, tote bag or *VBS 2023 Backpack* (9781087776606), cardboard blocks

- Place a copy of the "Bible Verse Marker" (pack item 7) in each Bible at Psalm 107:1. Hide the Bibles around the room. Lay one Bible on the floor and cover with the "Color Gameboard" (pack item 25). Slip a Bible in the bag and place to one side on the floor. Cover a Bible with the cardboard blocks. Place one under a crib and cover it with a blanket.
- Sing "Play a Game" (Music and Movement Tab). Tell the child that she can play a game and search for the Bible.
- Clap when she finds a Bible. She can turn the pages or find another place to "hide" the Bible.
- When a child opens a Bible to the marker, read the verse. Say: "God loves us."

## USE GEL BAGS

**Supplies:** "Puzzles" (pack item 26), homemade gel bags (see "Gel Bag Games" [pack item 23]), scissors

- Make gel bags as directed on "Gel Bag Games" (pack item 23). Cut two or three of the "Puzzles" (pack item 26) one in half with one straight cut. Arrange items on the floor with other toys.
- Lay a gel bag in front of a child. Press on the gel bag gently and encourage the child to do the same.
- Find the object inside the bag. Press around the object to make it move along the gameboard.
- Say: "God made everything. God made people. People can use their hands. You can use your hands."
- Help a child find two pieces that make a picture. Look at the picture. Say: "These children are playing together. You play with your friends at VBS."

## PAINT ON A GAMEBOARD

**Supplies:** "Large Gameboards" (pack item 24), paper, dot painters, trays; EXTEND: Watercolors, paintbrushes, painting smocks

- Make copies of the "Large Gameboards" (pack item 24) so each child will have one if he chooses.
- Place the gameboards, blank paper, and dot painters on a table or trays on the floor.
- Invite a child to use the dot painters to paint on a gameboard or a blank piece of paper.
- As children work, say: "God made everything. God made people. People can use their hands to work and play. Thank You, God, for making us."

**EXTEND:** As an additional or alternate activity, use watercolors and paintbrushes to paint the gameboards.

## PLAY A BASKET GAME

**Supplies:** "Jesus Cube" (pack item 15), "Animal Cube" (pack item 16), "Color Cube" (pack item 17), "Pattern Cube" (pack item 18), laundry basket, yarn, scissors, small foam or inflatable balls; EXTEND: Plastic animal figures

- Tie one end of the yarn to the side of the laundry basket. Weave yarn back and forth and across the laundry basket opening to create a "web." Tie the other end of the yarn to the basket. (Use several smaller lengths of yarn or one long length to make the web.) Leave the web open enough to reach your hand through the yarn and touch the bottom of the basket. Set the basket on the floor. Carefully place cubes and balls through the web into the bottom of the basket.
- Tap the edge of the laundry basket to get a child's attention. Sing "Play a Game" (Music & Movement Tab).
- Invite a child to reach through the web to retrieve one of the balls or cubes. Some children may find this challenging. Encourage their efforts and assist as needed. Supervise children closely so no one gets tangled or strangled.
- Suggest the children place the objects back in the basket as they retrieve them.
- Look at pictures on the cubes and talk about the animals or the story about Jesus. Name the colors on the "Color Cube" (pack item 17).
- Say: "God made everything. God sent Jesus. Thank You, God."

**EXTEND:** Add plastic animal figures that will fit inside the basket.

## COMPLETE PICTURE PUZZLES

**Supplies:** "Puzzles" (pack item 26), reusable lunch bag, tray, scissors, wooden puzzles

- Cut apart the "Puzzles" (pack item 26) and cut each one in half with one straight cut. Place one piece of each puzzle in the bag and the other piece on the tray. Set the bag on the floor with the tray beside it. Arrange other puzzles nearby.
- Invite a child to pull a puzzle piece from the bag. Challenge her to find the connecting piece and assemble the puzzle. Talk about the picture.
- As the child works, say: "These children are working and playing together. We get to work and play together at VBS."

## EXPLORE I-SPY BOTTLES AND BAGS

**Supplies:** Plastic drink bottles, sand, unpopped popcorn, small game pieces, small plastic number cubes, small interlocking bricks, buttons, pom-poms, glue, tape, homemade gel bags (see "Gel Bag Games" [pack item 23])

- Make I-Spy bottles. Fill some bottles about ¾ with sand. Drop in some number cubes and game pieces. Shake to hide the items in the sand. Fill other bottles about ¾ full of popcorn. Drop in some buttons, pom-poms, and interlocking bricks. Seal the lids of all bottles with glue and tape.
- Make gel bags using the instructions on "Gel Bag Games" (pack item 23). Drop 2–3 game pieces in each gel bag. Seal the openings of the bags with tape.
- Invite preschoolers to turn, shake, and move the bottles. Challenge them to identify what they see inside the bottles.
- Show a preschooler how to press on the gel bag to find and move the game pieces.
- Say: "We learn and have fun at VBS. We can learn about God. God loves and cares for you."
- Sing "God Loves and Cares" (Music & Movement Tab).

## PAINT WITH NUMBER CUBES

**Supplies:** "Large Gameboards" (pack item 24), paper, oatmeal box with lid, number cubes, blue paint in a cup, spoons, scissors, masking tape

- Make copies of the "Large Gameboards" (pack item 24). Roll up the paper and cut it to fit inside the oatmeal box.
- Slide the paper into the box. Help a child drop a cube into paint. Scoop out the covered cube with a spoon and drop into the box. Put the lid on the box; seal with a strip of tape over the lid.
- Invite the child to shake and roll the oatmeal box or roll it back and forth with the child. Talk about the sound you hear (the number cube in the box).
- Say: "We have heard stories about God. God loves us and cares for us."
- Open the box and pull out the paper. Talk about the colors and lines you see. Place the painting aside to dry.

## MOVE ANIMALS ON A GAME PATH

**Supplies:** Several trays or large pieces of paper, large plastic animal figures

- Place the trays (or paper) side by side to create a game path. Place the animals at one end of the path.
- Sing "Play a Game" (Music and Movement Tab) and clap your hands as you sit near the game path.
- Move one of the animal figures onto the first tray. Encourage a preschooler to move the animal down the path, onto the next tray (or further).
- Say: "We can play a game with the animals." Encourage the child to name the animals.
- Say: "God made all the animals. God made everything."

**EXTEND:** If using paper for the game path, suggest that the preschoolers step from space to space, too.

DAYS 1–5

## MAKE A COLLAGE

**Supplies:** "Game Cards Printable" (pack item 19), "Bible Verse Markers" (pack item 7), colored heavyweight paper, roll of prize tickets, game cards collected from board or card games, clear contact plastic, scissors, trays (optional)
EXTEND: Paper

- Make copies of "Game Cards Printable" (pack item 19) and "Bible Verse Markers" (pack item 7) on colored heavyweight paper. Cut the cards apart. Cut some or all of the cards into halves or thirds. Pull apart several of the prize tickets. Cut the old game cards into halves. Cut a few squares or triangles of blank colored paper.
- Cut a 5-inch square of contact plastic. Lay the contact plastic on a table or tray with the sticky side up.
- Invite a child to press game card and paper pieces to the sticky paper to create a collage.
- Name the colors of paper as a child presses a card on his collage.
- As a child presses a Bible verse onto the sticky plastic, point to the words. Say: "These are the words of our Bible verse. 'God loves us.' We have been learning about God's love in VBS. God loves and cares for you."
- When a child finishes his collage, peel backing from another piece of contact plastic and press over the collage (to seal in all the remaining sticky areas). Trim the edges as needed.

**✱ EXTEND:** Help a preschooler glue a few game cards or paper squares onto pages 14–15 of the Keepsake Book. Older twos may enjoy using glue sticks to make collages on paper instead of contact plastic.

## SCOOP AND POUR

**Supplies:** Dishpan or plastic bin, checkers, plastic drink lids, counting chips, game pieces and tokens, animal counters or animal figures, cups, large scoops, *2023 VBS Music for Babies–2s*

- Place all the objects in the dishpan or bin and mix them. Set the dishpan on the floor with the cups and scoops.
- Invite a child to scoop and pour the objects. Older twos may begin to sort the items by color or type.
- Play "Twists and Turns" while the preschoolers work.
- Say: "We learn about God and the Bible at VBS."
- When a child finds an animal, recall one of the Bible stories with animals.
- Supervise children closely as some items may present choking hazards.

## PLAY A COLOR GAME

**Supplies:** "Color Cube" (pack item 17), "Color Gameboard" (pack item 25), baby toys; EXTEND: "Sorting Cards" (pack item 10), "Puzzles" (pack item 26)

- Gather baby toys that match each of the six colors on the "Color Cube." Place the toys around the room or use toys already in the room.
- Hand the cube to a child and lead him to toss the cube onto the floor.
- Point to the color and name it. Ask the children to find toys that are the same color as this one.
- When children bring back toys, place them on the appropriate color space on the gameboard.
- After gathering a few toys, guide preschoolers to take the toys and return them to different areas of the room before rolling and playing the game again.
- Say: "God made a beautiful world full of colors. God made everything."

**EXTEND:** Lay the "Sorting Cards" (pack item 10) and "Puzzles" (pack item 26) beside the gameboard; lay them with the color sides up. Encourage older twos to sort the cards onto the gameboard. For pieces with more than one color, match it to either space on the board.

## ARRANGE FACE GAME CARDS

**Supplies:** "Instructions" (pack item 20), materials to make a felt board, "It's You! Faces" (pack item 11), "It's You! Frames" (pack item 21), felt pieces or rough side of Velcro®, other felt shapes or felt-backed figures, camera

- Make a felt board as directed in "Instructions" (pack item 20). Take photos of the children. Make copies of "It's You! Frames" (pack item 21) and attach children's pictures to the frames. Attach felt or rough Velcro to the backs of these photos and to the "It's You! Faces" (pack item 11). Place the faces and the other felt items near the felt board.
- Invite preschoolers to place the faces and shapes on the felt board. They can arrange them as they choose.
- As children put items on the board and take them off, pick up one of the photos. Say: "Look! It's our friend, _____ (insert child's name). God loves _____. God loves you."
- Encourage older twos to create a design on the felt board with the shapes and faces.

**EXTEND:** Add photos of the children to pages 8–9 of the Keepsake Books.

## LINE UP TOYS

**Supplies:** "Animal Pairs" (pack item 13), "Jesus Cube" (pack item 15), "Animal Cube" (pack item 16), "Color Cube" (pack item 17), "Pattern Cube" (pack item 18), painter's tape, small boxes, large interlocking blocks, other toys

- Use tape to create wavy or zigzag lines on the floor. Tape "Animal Pairs"(item 13) to small boxes so they will stand.
- Set one of the toys or animal pairs on the tape line.
- Invite preschoolers to add additional toys along the tape line, filling up the path.
- Say: "We can work together to fill the line. We also work together to learn at VBS. We can learn about God while we play and have fun."

## DRAW ON A SPINNER

**Supplies:** Paper, washable markers, lazy Susan turntable, tape

- Cut paper to fit on the turntable. Attach one piece of paper to the turntable with a small roll of tape.
- Sit beside the spinner and gently turn the turntable.
- When a child shows interest, invite him to spin the turntable gently.
- While the child turns the turntable, remove the lid from a marker and touch the paper to make a line as the turntable spins.
- Suggest the child hold the marker while you spin the turntable.
- When a child wants to move to another area, make sure to retrieve the marker. Tell preschoolers that markers must stay near the turntable.

**✱ EXTEND:** Suggest a child draw his family (or make marks) on page 5 of the Keepsake Book. Say: "God made your family. Thank You, God."

## 1s AND 2s LOVE TO MOVE AND THEY LOVE MUSIC.

Music and movement can be used to teach, to comfort or stimulate a child, and to encourage group participation. Try these ideas for incorporating music and movement into the VBS session:

- Sing or play music and move around the room with an upset child.
- Play musical instruments while waiting for a turn or while waiting for parents.
- March to music to burn energy before a quiet activity. Challenge older 2s and younger 3s to play a simple musical instrument while marching. (Note: This is a difficult skill for most 1s and 2s.)
- Use songs to help teach and reinforce Bible truths.
- Use music in place of conversation. Example: Don't just say the Bible verse, sing it instead!
- Play music quietly in the background as children play.
- Wave fabric streamers to music while leading children to move around the room.
- Play calming music quietly during nap or rest times. Sing simple songs to familiar tunes such as "Mary Had a Little Lamb" (see reverse side).

# MUSIC & MOVEMENT

# BIBLE-TEACHING SONGS AND ACTIVITY SONG

## GOD LOVES AND CARES
Tune: *"Farmer in the Dell"*

God loves and cares for me*
God loves and cares for me
I learn from the Bible that
God loves and cares for me

*Substitute children's names in the song.

## LEARN ABOUT GOD
Tune: *"God Is So Good"*

Learn about God
Learn about God
Learn about God
Learn from the Bible

## PLAY A GAME
Tune: *"Mary Had a Little Lamb"*

Come and play a game with me
Play a game, play a game
Come and play a game with me
Play a game with friends

## THANK YOU, GOD
Tune: *"Happy Birthday"*

Thank You, God, for the sun*
Thank You, God, for the sun
Thank You, God, for loving us
Thank You, God, for the sun

*Substitute other things God made; or substitute the children's names.

## UP AND DOWN
Tune: *"Twinkle, Twinkle Little Star"*

Up and down and up and down
Move your scarf now, up and down
Way up high and way down low
Over your head and by your toes
Up and down and up and down
Move your scarf now, up and down

## TWISTS AND TURNS

Spin the spinner
Beat the clock
Skip ahead, go again,
Level up, play to win
Give it all you've got!

Take the challenge
Make your move
Ready, set, here we go
Jesus will let us know
What we need to do

(Chorus)
Twists and Turns
Twists and Turns
Following Jesus changes the game
Twists and Turns

He will guide us
All the way
Every up, every down
Jesus will help us out
Each and every day

(Repeat Chorus)
Make your ways known to me, LORD
Teach me your paths

Make your ways known to me, LORD
Teach me your paths
(REPEAT)

(Repeat Chorus 2x)

Twists and Turns
Twists and Turns

Words and music by Paul Marino and Jeremy Johnson. Arranged by Paul Marino and Jeremy Johnson. © Copyright 2022 Van Ness Press, Inc. (ASCAP) (admin. by Lifeway Worship c/o Music Services, www.musicservices.org). All rights reserved. Used by permission. CCLI#7198369.

## GOD MADE WONDERFUL THINGS

God made wonderful things
God made wonderful things
The flowers, the animals, trees and grass
God made wonderful things
God made wonderful things
God made wonderful things
The sun and the moon and the stars that shine
God made wonderful things

Words and music by Wayne Tester. © Copyright 2010 Van Ness Press, Inc. (ASCAP) (admin. by Lifeway Worship c/o Music Services, www.musicservices.org). All rights reserved. Used by permission. CCLI#5648342.

## I CAN SEE GOD'S WORLD

I can see God's world
I can see God's world
With my eyes I can see the clear blue sky
I can see God's world

I can hear God's world
I can hear God's world
With my ears I can hear the chirping birds
I can hear God's world

I can touch God's world
I can touch God's world
With my hand I can touch the animals fur
I can touch God's world

I can taste God's world
I can taste God's world
With my mouth I can taste the yummy food
I can taste God's world

I can smell God's world
I can smell God's world
With my nose I can smell the fresh spring flowers
I can smell God's world

I can see God's world
I can see God's world
With my eyes I can see the clear blue sky
I can see God's world

Words and music by Esther Maus-Tester. © Copyright 2011 McKinney Music, Inc. (BMI) (admin. by Lifeway Worship c/o Music Services, www.musicservices.org). All rights reserved. Used by permission. CCLI#5919909.

## FAMILIES LOVE

Families love and families care
Families learn to help and give
I'm a big part of my family
Yes, I'm a big part of my family

Words and music by Esther Maus-Tester. © Copyright 2011 McKinney Music, Inc. (BMI) (admin. by Lifeway Worship c/o Music Services, www.musicservices.org). All rights reserved. Used by permission. CCLI#5919899.

## I AM SAFE

When I am afraid
I know Jesus loves me
When I'm feeling scared
I know He is there

(Chorus)
Even in the storms
The thunder and the lightning
Sometimes can be frightening
But I know He's beside me
And I am safe

When I am afraid
I know Jesus loves me
When I'm feeling scared
I know He is there

(Repeat Chorus 2x)

Words and music by Paul Marino and Jeremy Johnson. Arranged by Paul Marino and Jeremy Johnson. © Copyright 2022 Van Ness Press, Inc. (ASCAP) (admin. by Lifeway Worship c/o Music Services, www.musicservices.org). All rights reserved. Used by permission. CCLI#7198308.

## SPECIAL JESUS (TESTRICITY*)

(Chorus)
Special Jesus, special Jesus
Born in Bethlehem.
Special Jesus, special Jesus
Come and worship Him

In a manger for a bed
Baby Jesus laid His Head
Special Jesus, special Jesus
Come and worship Him

(Repeat Chorus)

Peace on earth the angels sing
Glory to God's Son, the King
Special Jesus, special Jesus,
Come and worship Him.

All is calm and all is bright
On this silent, holy night
Special Jesus, special Jesus,
Come and worship Him.
Come and worship Him.

Words and music by Esther Maus-Tester and Wayne Tester. © Copyright 2014 McKinney Music, Inc. (BMI)/Van Ness Press, Inc. (ASCAP) (admin. by Lifeway Worship c/o Music Services, www.musicservices.org). All rights reserved. Used by permission. CCLI #7024785. *www.TESTRICITY.com.

## JESUS LOVES ALL PEOPLE THE SAME

Jesus loves all people the same
Jesus loves all people the same
He knows who we are and He knows our names
Jesus loves all people the same

(Repeat)

(Chorus)
Jesus, He loves everyone
Oh yes He does
Jesus, He loves
You and me!

Jesus loves all people the same
Jesus loves all people the same
He knows who we are and He knows our names
Jesus loves all people the same
(Repeat Chorus)

Jesus loves all people the same
Jesus loves all people the same
He knows who we are and He knows our names
Jesus loves all people the same

Words and music by Paul Marino and Jeremy Johnson. Arranged by Paul Marino and Jeremy Johnson. © Copyright 2022 Van Ness Press, Inc. (ASCAP) (admin. by Lifeway Worship c/o Music Services, www.musicservices.org). All rights reserved. Used by permission. CCLI#7198310.

## TWIST LIKE THIS

It's time to move
It's time to groove
It's time to show everybody
What you can do

Twist ... like this
Twist ... like this
Now bob your head ... like this
Then twist ... like this

(Chorus)
Step to the left
Step to the right
Now spin around
Put your hands up high

(Repeat)
And twist ... like this
Everybody twist ... like this
Now bob your head ... like this
And twist ... like this

(Repeat Chorus)

Now twist ... like this
Twist ... like this
Now bob your head ... like this
Everybody twist ... like this

Words and music by Paul Marino and Jeremy Johnson. Arranged by Paul Marino and Jeremy Johnson. © Copyright 2022 Van Ness Press, Inc. (ASCAP) (admin. by Lifeway Worship c/o Music Services, www.musicservices.org). All rights reserved. Used by permission. CCLI#7198316.